SHADOWS & SUPPOSES

Also by Gloria Vando

Promesas: Geography of the Impossible

SHADOWS & SUPPOSES

Gloria Vando

Winner of the Poetry Society of America's 1998 Alice Fay di Castagnola Award

Arte Público Press
Houston, Texas

This volume is made possible through grants from the National Endowment for the Arts and the City of Houston through The Cultural Arts Council of Houston, Harris County.

Recovering the past, creating the future

Arte Público Press
University of Houston
452 Cullen Performance Hall
Houston, Texas 77204-2004

Cover art: Ruth Thorne-Thomsen, "Thunderhead, Views from the Shoreline, Colorado, 1986," courtesy of the Laurence Miller Gallery, New York

Cover design by Giovanni Mora

Vando, Gloria.
Shadows & Supposes / by Gloria Vando.
p. cm.
"Winner of the Poetry Society of America's 1998 Alice Fay di Castagnola Award."
ISBN 1-55885-360-X (pbk. : alk. paper)
1. Title: Shadows and Supposes. II. Title.
PS3572.A67 S53 2002
811′.54—dc21 2001056721
CIP

∞ The paper used in this publication meets the requirements of the American National Standard for Information Sciences—Permanence of Paper for Printed Library Materials, ANSI Z39.48-1984.

Printed in the United States of America

2 3 4 5 6 7 8 9 0 1 10 9 8 7 6 5 4 3 2 1

Contents

III

IV

To my mother, Anita Velez-Mitchell,
my children, Lorca, Paul, and Anika,
and my Wild Bill

Acknowledgments

The author wishes to thank Ann Slegman, David Ray, Robert Stewart, and her family for their thoughtful reading and suggestions; MultiStages for creating a beautiful and stirring theatre piece from three of her poems; Sheila Seck for her generous legal assistance; and the editors of the following magazines and anthologies in which some of these poems first appeared, sometimes in different versions.

American Diaspora: Poetry of Exile (Iowa Press, 2001); *Carolina Quarterly; City Life; Cottonwood* ("Gloria Vando Issue"); *Floricanto Sí! Contemporary U.S. Latina Poetry* (Penguin USA, 1997); *Like Thunder: Poets Respond to Violence in America* (Iowa Press, 2002); *Luna Magazine; The Mid-America Poetry Review; Movieworks Anthology* (Little Theatre Press, 1990); *New Letters; Paper Dance: 55 Latino Poets* (Persea Books, 1995); *River Styx; Spud Songs: An Anthology of Potato Poems* (Helicon Nine Editions, 1999); *Stiletto One; Touching the Fire: 15 Poets of Today's Latino Renaissance* (Anchor/Doubleday, 1999); *Uncle; Visualizing Poetry* (SAS Institute, 1999); *Western Humanities Review; Writing Poems,* 5th ed. (Addison Wesley Longman, 2000).

"Cloverleaf and Other Food for Thought" was presented on "New Letters on the Air" (KCUR-FM) on 11/25/99.

"Vietnam/Burn Imagery" and "Lydia's Phantasmagoria" were adapted for the stage as a one-act play titled, "Moving Targets: Three Interpretations of Murder," and presented by MultiStages at the Phil Bosakowski Theatre in New York City.

"On Hearing that a Potato Costs $70 in Sarajevo" won a prize in the 1997 *River Styx* International Poetry Contest (Philip Levine, judge).

Caprichos, a chapbook (*Stiletto*, Howling Dog Press, 1989), contains four of the poems included in this collection.

“And tell me those are shadows and supposes.”
(King John to Matilda)
—Michael Drayton, *England’s Heroical Epistles*

Loss and possession, death and life are one,
There falls no shadow where there shines no sun.
—Hilaire Belloc, “For a Sundial”

I

Almighty God, Father of all mercies, we pray Thee to be gracious with those who fly this night. Guard and protect those of us who venture out into the darkness of Thy heaven. Uphold them on Thy wings. Keep them safe both in body and soul and bring them back to us. Give to us all the courage and strength for the hours that are ahead; give to them rewards according to their efforts. Above all else, our Father, bring peace to Thy world. May we go forward trusting in Thee and knowing we are in Thy presence now and forever. Amen.

—Prayer by Chaplain Downey, ending the briefing session preliminary to the bombing of Nagasaki

¿Pero qué sucedió? Sentimos
bajo los pies algo que huía
y que nos hacía caer.

Era la sangre de este siglo.

—Pablo Neruda

Flag Day at Union Cemetery

I enter the clearing
the way we sometimes enter dreams,
the door to the afternoon
clicking behind me,
caution setting like a sun.

On my own, I stand in the center
of this hard-edged lawn,
dwarfed and domed
by a neutered sky, and wonder
how long it would take to turn
me into stone, dust, song—
a process rousing itself
with every incarnation.

When we were children, we'd
whirl each other around,
our skirts unfurling
like these 5,000 banners
waving from the dead—
then we'd let go

and each spun form
would freeze at a command,
breath and laughter chiseled
into pillars, like the headstones here—
exclamations marking
each life's absurd spin, guffawing
in perfect unison,
in perfect deadly rows.

—for Tim Barnhart

On Hearing that a Potato Costs $70 in Sarajevo

*—in memory of SPUD: Society
for the Prevention of Unhealthy Diets*

Potato: for want of it the Irish invaded Boston,
Suffolk County, maybe even Maine, before
settling into a life of slim-trim resignation,
replicating hometown farms, starch swelling
the landscape in mounds the shape of potatoes—
did they in fact make it to Idaho, or was that
another hungry invasion, or was it coincidence,
the commonwealth of cuisine?—no matter,
they would always be paired with that symbol
of nagging contradictions served up in dual images
of gluttony and starvation, frailty and pollution
(the first insecticide having been invented
to prevent the blight of the potato beetle—
a contradiction in itself, with its black and yellow
stripes camouflaging a pinprick of a mouth
that would devour whole undersides of leaves in
picoseconds, and its equally disarming orange-yellow
eggs clustered like tiny land mines set to explode
at deadly intervals—and just this morning
I was reading a loud black and yellow *WARNING!*
about its pesticidal progeny: *this* -zine and *that* -zine
poisoning our mid-western streams, our drinking
water, our *children,* for godssake—leaving nothing
for us to do but move back to Boston, Suffolk
County, and points east); potato as victim and
victimizer, like the Irish themselves, trapped
in the Belfast of the human condition, the torn
war zone of the heart, a people whose namesake
is the jig, the wake, and the potato, the Irish potato—

even though its zigzag journey started in Peru,
crossing the Atlantic in the deep hull of Spanish
shame, where some poor slob of a galley slave
found himself *jodido* through centuries of KP;
even though all of Europe thrived on it through
two world wars, and the neutral nations of Benelux
(*Nazis? where? where?*) craved it and carved it
on their plates with gusto and a kind of reverence
for its neutral flavor—I know this firsthand,
the rest I read in the third or fourth edition
of the *Columbia Encyclopedia,* which I cross-
referenced with my Nisei friend Eddy Iino,
soon after I returned from Amsterdam, where
my schoolmate Denise, a hefty ballerina, once
invited me to dinner, a pleasant surprise since
the Dutch were still listing from the unexpected
Nazi wallop and some said her father was ill,
the SS screaming nightly obscenities in his dreams,
so ill he'd had to resign from the University—
foolish, weak man, they said, the war was over, over,
you had to get on with your life, wear your
shirtsleeves long, tightly buttoned at the wrist,
never, *never* view your body in the mirror, that's
what any sane person would do, they said—
and that evening the Delft china and sterling were
laid out for Denise's friend, crystal water goblets
reflecting the pink and purple petals of the tulips
from my garden, and Mrs. Van Beek, in a demure
v-necked navy blue dress, nodded and smiled
at me, her first guest since World War II, and
gently—oh so gently—doled out helping after
helping of unaccompanied peeled, boiled, and
quartered potatoes—*a tuber sonata!*—while

the rest of us (carefully skirting Van Gogh),
discussed deStijl, Pater, Piet Mondrian, and—
Oh yes, Professor Van Beek asked, *have you seen*
the queen's photograph in the paper?—Wilhelmina
sloshing heroically through floodwaters of the low
lowlands, the soggy weight of her hem revealing
the residue of nightshade on her regal buttocks—
and did you hear Prince Bernhardt extolling the virtues
of Volendam on the radio?—his actual words now
muffled by the enduring properties of starch
gluing my host's tongue to the roof of his mouth
so that Prince Bernhardt, hero though he was,
produced merely an inarticulate phlegmy growl—
nngkhggnngchgnnngggrrachkkrchrecggrr—a jarring
characteristic of Dutch, with or without
potatoes—*aardappelen*—earth's apples (as opposed
to heaven's, where Spanish jokes about *la papa,*
el Papa, and *el papá* would never circulate)—
earth's apples, wearing a dull and dirty post-
Edenic coat, this time, to help poor Adam ("man"
in Hebrew) resist temptation: there's just no biting
into a raw potato; it's got to be peeled, cooked,
blinded—thereby affording Adam an unobserved
hour or two to think things over: the potato, not
unlike an unloaded gun by the bed or an unhoned
knife in the kitchen, gives one pause, a chance
to look around, reflect, choose one's arena
with care: a woman, they say, kills in the kitchen
(a sharp blade to his gut), a man in the bed (twisted
linens knotted at her throat), but in other rooms
of the human house, where bare hands reign,
our only recourse is to put ours together and pray
for a deterrent—a sudden surge of arthritis or
peripheral neuropathy or impotence, any of which

can be suppressed with megadoses of mincrals,
abundant in the skins of the coveted, ubiquitous,
though sometimes unaffordable potato.

---

jodido—"screwed"
el Papa—the Pope
la papa—the potato
el papá—the daddy

The Cloverleaf & Other Food for Thought

I stuff the leftover turkey
into the disposal, the giblets
and gravy sliding thickly
off the plate, and wonder
how many children could feast
on what I casually reject.

This evening, a dinner guest
from Hong Kong, who now makes
a lot of bread as a stockbroker
with Merrill Lynch and is married
to a systems engineer adept at
feeding data into computers,
remembers how she once watched
beggars outside her window
fighting over her discarded
banana peel. It was 1946,
she explains. Food was scarce.
Only Macao, a Portuguese colony
that remained neutral (to all moral
issues) survived the war.

When I was growing up I had to eat
everything on my plate because
they were starving in Poland.
During my mother's generation
they were starving in Armenia.
Yesterday they were starving
in Ethiopia, today Zaire. Notice
how they always pick exotic
places. Too far away to visit.
Too far away to hear. A small cry
on the other side of the freeway.

Gaetano, Roma, 1955

He tells her he loves her,
this dark little man who hates so much.
He says he can tell at once
who is, who isn't,
that he could never love one of *them.*
How could he? A black shirt.
A poet. Mussolini's poet.
Writing odes to glory,
Il Duce, to Aryan beauty,
this dark little man with
a smudged moustache, leaning
toward her on the grass, his mouth
reaching for hers. She turns
her head, feels his face
in her blonde hair, his lips
on her neck, his well-versed hand
on her breast. *Tesoro,* he sighs,
mio tesoro. I will get you
a scholarship to study art
in Sienna—the best school
in the world. But she has turned
her back on him, on Italy, on Bernini,
numbers burning themselves
into her arm, a yellow star
leading her home.

Museum of Natural History, Munich

I loved the great whale most,
its zeppelin body large enough to jail
a disbeliever far below the depths
of faith, turning his world upside down
until in giddy confusion he'd recant,
emerging (with a rude shove from
his host) upright, righteous,
a noble specimen—mankind.
Here in this marble hall, the dirigible
floats like an omen or an advertisement
high above a sea of gaping mouths,
my children's and my own among them:
I have brought them here to my
childhood school for lofty reasons,
as my mother once brought me.
Like bees they flit from flora to fauna
in one wing of this grand scheme
of still, still life. I promise to return
each day of our stay until they see it all,
but now it's time to go. At a nod,
the two youngest are off in two directions.
Lorca and I set out to find them. I spot
Paul hiding behind a hippopotamus
and Anika crouched beneath the testicles
of a yak—but now Lorca is missing
from this room, and the next.
I stop an old woman, *Habensie ein*
kleines kind gese—She stares my voice
down to a stutter and struts away.
An unfamiliar sound makes me turn—
amidst a forest of four-legged creatures,
I see my lost child, her small hands

stroking the neck of a fawn, her cheek wet
against its cheek, lips to ear,
poor thing, poor little thing.

Vietnam/Burn Imagery Transcript

—for Huynh Cong Ut

Viet War Photo Challenged;
Westmoreland Says Hibachi,
Not Napalm, Burned Girl
—The Washington Post

1.
They come at you like shrapnel
lodging themselves into your throat,
come at you as though blown from the photo,
hurtling toward you as toward the cameraman,
who in that instant must choose
between saving five little bodies and
salving his conscience or

capturing an image that will ignite
the conscience of the world.

He shoots.

I want you to get comfortable
put all of your thoughts away
close your eyes . . . relax and listen

Bringing up the rear, four soldiers
in pursuit or also fleeing—who knows?—
this is a time of mixed metaphors:
good begets bad and vice versa.

let each count be a signal to relax
as I count down from ten to one

The oldest child, a boy of ten

nine . . . eight . . . seven . . . six . . .

springs from the bottom left corner of the picture
as if into your arms, his face contorted
like an ancient tragic mask.

more and more relaxed now . . .
five . . . four . . .

Hardly three, the smallest child looks back
at the dense cloud enshrouding
her village, looks back
for the last time, her youth, her past, all past
obliterated in two anonymous clicks:

all war compressed into one still frame.

relax your feet now, letting
them get warm, comfortable, heavy

On the right, her sister, dainty in terror,
pulling their baby brother by the hand,
lava scalding their heels.

And, in the center, the one you first see
but dare not see, pushing her image aside
until you can catch your breath—

relax, release the tension in your stomach
let all tightness go out of your chest

there, in the center, the girl, the little girl
naked, melting, her arms
extended from her body like a modern Christ,
her scream hurtling through the air like a buzz bomb,

at the count of three
let go of any tension you may still have

one . . . two . . . three . . .

a scream, the photographer and
the nineteen-year-old boy, who circles overhead
to witness what he has unleashed, will hear
like a mournful epilogue night after night,

whenever you feel anxious
say to yourself: relax, calm, peace

a scream imprinted in their brains,
passed on to coming generations
as long as the brain can recreate itself.

2.
The pilot is thirty-nine now, recently wed. Maybe
a victim of Agent Orange. He wonders. Relieved
of active duty in Nam, he received an honorable
discharge, medals, and body-mending from the military.

the burned skin that is no longer alive
needs to be rubbed off so new skin can grow

First year back he soundlessly stalks
the midline of streets, wary
of ambushes, of snipers braided into the gnarled
branches of the giant oaks that line his block.
Soft-stirring leaves mar his peripheral peace,
sudden sharp sounds send him sprawling

cool cream is put on your burns
it feels good as it touches your skin

and always he senses a presence stalking him,
    hiding beneath parked cars, lurking
    in lampless doorways, down alleys,

under bushes—wherever the jungle thickens.

Always alert. Always awake. Always at war.

close your eyes, take a deep breath
stay calm, and let the moment pass

Years later they are still after him.
It is a given. Like death.

now picture yourself well, healthy
in the most beautiful place imaginable

In his dreams where their roles reverse each night,
it is his child—the one he longs for but cannot have—
his child running naked down Oak Street,
her seared flesh flapping against her small bones,
her arms like a wounded fledgling, reaching for him.

Note: Italicized sections are based on the Burn Imagery Transcript, which is used in the treatment of burn victims.

blood tax

he packs carefully, placing
between two undershirts
a recent photograph
of his mother and father
his three sisters, his brother
and himself, all cornered
self-consciously
in a gilded Woolworth frame

mambrú se fue a la guerra

he adds a rosary,
a memorial card
for his *abuelita* (1910–1965),
with the 23rd Psalm,
printed in unevenly spaced
gold letters on the back

qué dolor

and the Virgin Mary,
arms extended in supplication,
on the face

qué dolor

next, the Spanish *Bible* he received
for his first communion,
a comb and brush set from graduation,
a toenail clipper,
an envelope with photomatic
pictures of his girl kissing him
on the lips

qué pena

a baseball mitt—
changes his mind and
flings it disdainfully

across the room—kid stuff

mambrú se fue a la guerra

his mother enters wordlessly,
sobbing despite her vow,
places four neatly rolled pairs
of matched socks on the pillow
beside the open valise
and stands by the bed watching him,
wanting to stroke his bent back,
to hold him in her arms

y no sé cuándo vendrá

he does not look up,
but raises the volume
on his new Sony Walkman,

que do re mi
que do re fa

its manly commands
drowning out her sorrow

no sé si volverá

---

blood tax—Although Puerto Ricans are citizens of the United States (Puerto Rico is a colony), they do not pay federal income tax or have representation in Congress. They are, however, conscripted into the Armed Forces. Puerto Ricans suffered a great number of casualties during the Vietnam War.

mambrú se fué a la guerra…— "Mambrú has gone to war/ what pain, what pain, what sorrow/ Mambrú has gone to war/ and I don't know when he'll come back/ *que do re mi/ que do re fa/* I don't know if he'll come back." "Mambrú," a popular children's song in Puerto Rico, is a corruption of the French ditty, "*Malbrouck s'en va-t-en guerre.*"

*Desen*canto

Ezra Pound was arrested for treason
fifty years ago today. This poet
who shaped the art for the rest
(the best) of us speaks to me now
on my car radio. In a familiar voice
that could be selling beer or cigarettes
or forecasting tomorrow's weather
he calls for the execution of
"100 yids for every fascist soldier slain."
His words stall my heart.

—for Karl Shapiro

Desencanto—disenchantment

On This Day I Think of the Widows
February 14th

On this day I think of the widows
who awoke before dawn and planned
a morning of strenuous exercise,
five times around the mall
until the stores open, then new
linens for the bed, a down pillow
or two, scented paper for
the closet empty in the hall.
An afternoon of cleaning windows
and attics, discarding clothes
snug to the point of pain.

On this day I think of the widows
who busy themselves in kitchens,
clanging pots and pans like tocsins
warding off despair, who dedicate
an hour before tea to scouring
grease off burners on the stove,
who fall to their knees, as in prayer,
and wax each linoleum square
until it glows and they can see
reflected in its speckled gray their
own neglected faces.

On this day I think of the widows,
my friends, who fall asleep exhausted
at day's end, the television hawking
its relentless, heartless lie.

Wind Chill Factor

—for Daisy Rhau

You point to a photo of your family
taken after they fled from North Korea,
your infant mother in her father's arms,
despots pursuing them the way Uncle Sam
pursued my grandparents after confiscating
their power, their land, its yield of sugar
and coffee, iron and ore, giving them
three weeks—always three weeks!—
to relocate. Before the exodus

your mother awoke each morning
in a tepid bath, her sleeping body phased
into a basin of wrist-warm water to lessen
the shock of life, the anticipated march across
the wide divide between privilege and
anonymity—snipers, land mines at every turn.

As a child I awoke to tepid clothes,
my grandmother warming each tiny garment
with her body—my socks running a low
temperature under each arm, my panties
wedged in her cleavage, my shirtsleeves
embracing her neck, her whole body
a conduit of early morning comfort
as she dressed me under the covers,
easing me into the glare of indifference,
then rage, against an alien shade or sound.

She taught me to braid my hair, gathering
the three strands, like warring factions,
between her fingers, plaiting them over and
under and over and under until a perfect braid
emerged, my world in safe and tidy harmony.

Grown up, I wear my hair in a bun, the skill
of my grandmother's hands in mine,
weaving then coiling the long thin braid
into a perfect circle at the nape of my neck,
insulating me, still, against the chill.

Crossings

They bombed the Mostar today,
an ancient bridge in Bosnia,
smoothed by centuries of pedestrians

crossing the river. When I crossed it
years ago, I had to hang on
with both hands—one to the railing,

the other to my husband's
extended grip—to keep from
slipping off its marble-slick incline,

so slick it reminds me now
of Saint Peter's bronze statue,
the toes eroded by millions

of caressing hands crossing
that threshold of faith—a foot
I vowed I would not touch, but did—

and this war, *all* wars, suddenly
ambushed by two abraded images:
one small bridge, one little foot.

—for Pat Breed

Perennials

. . . Lares, Belfast, Kent State, Soweto, Managua,
Beirut, Tianenman Square . . .

The faces interchange, blur like a garden
of prized flowers caught in a hurricane—
ocher and white, peach and sienna—
twisting and crumpling in the squall
until one hue consumes them, and all
that you can see for miles around is red—

spurting everywhere like a sprinkler system
gone berserk, splattering benches, trees,
cheeks of women cycling home from work,
laundry sacks on their bent backs;

slapping the cries of children
trying to catch a glimpse of history,
catching instead a mouthful of death;

splotching the pen-clutched hand,
sketch pad, the lens of a hidden camera;
stinging the eyes of people centuries away
as they mourn the evening news, watch
crushed petals scatter in a surge of blood.

But mark my words: from this stained soil
a new variety will flourish—vibrant
as the sunflower, resilient as the mum,
vigilant as the cereus in the night,
and, like the orchid, so exquisite
it will shatter the resolve of tyrants.

II

"Everyone real or invented deserves
the open destiny of life."

—Grace Paley

Swallows of Salangan

> Morton Feldman Dies at 61;
> An Experimental Composer
> —*The New York Times*

Sixty-one? I thought you were that back
then when you first lumbered into our
lives "like a bear," my daughter said,
clutching hers and giving up her bed
without an argument. An owl, I thought,
observing two tufts of slick, brown hair
hanging free like weary horns; eyes intense,
intimidating, behind the thickest lenses
I had ever seen, then suddenly small,
glasses raised, scanning the inch-close
page with laser speed. It was summer
that March in Corpus Christi. A scent
of jasmine and moist tweed slipped past
you into the kitchen mingling at random
with the bacon and the coffee. Crumbs
from your lips added an aleatory voice
to the graph paper score you hummed:
you were making history at my breakfast
table and I, Clio, was feeding you honey.
Only your music was minimal. I was

impressed. Not only by your presence
but what you left with me, what stayed,
permeating the bones of memory until today
when I play your records at the library,
huge headphones holding pieces of the past
together in a vise of sound—sound, Morty,
your sound—disquieting, "getting
under the seat" as you had warned, yet
reverential, hushed, as if in mourning
for itself. Once, in Houston—remember?—

washes of that sound, a voix celeste
like a swell of keening swallows filled
the Rothko Chapel you honored, hallowing
the art, the chapel and all therein. Now
a scant two decades later, you are dead
and much is made of disillusion. But
it wasn't you or your music or the media
hype—perhaps the hype—that led
to disillusion, what my father maintained
is the worst thing that could happen.
Something sinister shortened America's
attention span to 30 screaming minutes,
the reading line to 19 picas, hemlines
to the crotch. This is a time of expedience,
of shrink-wrapped identical portions. No
foreplay. No afterthought. Get on with it.
And you, freed from "the intrinsic morality
of the medium," creating your own morality
with a four-and-one-half-hour string quartet
that ended to an almost empty hall—Ah,

where to preserve your innocence, Morty,
in a cage, under glass, the wolf at the door?
Had you forgotten that *4' 33"* of silence
was more than our culture could endure?
Even then, back then, my friend, when
you were Schubert to a flower generation.

Snowflakes

—for Elizabeth "Grandma" Layton

You hold up one last drawing
of an old Indian couple sitting
outside their tepee in the snow.
Their gray eyes hook me, draw me
into their drama, into their slow
ritual—the woman's hands knitting
booties for a child's child,
the man refining the arrowhead he
has carved for someone else's use.
In this culture, you explain, even
those condemned to death concern
themselves with life. They deal simply
and honestly with the body's decay.
They let go. This is the way
of their people; this is their way
of death. The two gray figures grow
so cold that each giant snowflake on
their shawls retains its perfect shape.
You say you mean them to be resigned,
but I see what they see. Beyond
the teepee, where it's warm, a dog's
eyes open yellow like a warning.
When I look back at you, past your
thick lenses, I see their eyes.
I tell you I want to kneel by
the old couple, hold them and keep
them warm until death comes.
Yes, even if the snowflakes melt.

Martha Belle's Fingers

—On the occasion of her 98th birthday,
30 September 1999

Martha Belle's fingers, ringed
with turquoise and silver,
clutch the air's imaginary gifts.
She waves them like enthused
antennae, as she speaks—
giving size to this huge thing
that delicate one, no thought
of concealing their cruel swell—
they are, she is.
Other bones inside her skin
keep time to her body's
ambitious rhythm, growing
as she shrinks. And I, beginning
my descent into that painful
hull, hide my fingers
beneath the table of our talk,
between the folds of my fear,
as Martha Belle's fingers sing.

Blanca's Red Lips

This wedding in Lawrence
is like most others except when it's over
the bride and groom get a standing
ovation, as if they were the ingenues
in a hit play with a happy ending.
An earlier wedding intrudes and I see
my friend Blanca jumping up and down
like a small child chanting *Yes! Yes!*
the groom's cheeks puffed with laughter,
the priest asking the congregation
to join him in a round of applause for
this special couple who, after ten years
of equivocating and playing the field,
chose to play it safe and get saved, *saved*—
and Blanca, her mouth a perfect oval of joy.
Then my sister's shower a year later,
the male stripper gyrating hips against air,
women snapping telephotos for a closer
look in the privacy of their own lens,
and Blanca, that same glaring smile,
ululating at his hard, false promise—
already knowing, even then knowing—
and we too busy asking tired questions
about babies and when, as though
we had a right to know, and just weeks
later Lorca's voice on the machine,
          sobbing, sobbing,
Blanca's red lips seared into my skin.

—for Blanca, who died of AIDS

Noche de Ronda

—In memory of Elvira Ríos

In Paris
they'd announce our arrival
by playing your song
and we'd all sing
the words in our shallow
high pitches
your voice ocean-deep
in our minds. Today I play
your records for my American
friends. They say
nice voice, but it means
nothing special to them—
and I, still aching
each time I find you
braided in my memories,
your Aztec hair sleeked back
into a tight fist,
your lips, a bright flower
staining the night,
the veil of cigarette smoke
unable to obscure
your eyes
or your song, Elvira, your song,
a dark whisper
in my heart telling me—
hija, it's going to be like this
always like this.

---

hija—daughter, child

Hands

My grandmother always turned her head away.
        ¡Ay Jesús! she would say,
        her hands like the wings of the Firebird
                shielding her eyes from
                the thieving instrument.

Why would you want an old woman on film?
        Una vieja casi muerta
        caught in the act of defying death, caged
                forever in this prison of self?
                Mala suerte, mala suerte.

And though I would hear the hiss of her fear
        and sense my wrongdoing,
        out of a desperate need to keep her
                from flight, I would persist
                in shooting.

On First Meeting the Poet

We were at the Prospect Restaurant in Kansas City
eating lunch with friends who had missed
the reading the night before, when as if on cue
the poet and his wife sauntered by
and we, delighted with our good fortune,
their good timing, rapped on the glass
and waved them in. And they came. He first,
teeth first, dimples belying the sternness
of the graying winter coat that covered one-quarter
of his face—but how can you be intimidated
by a guy who looks like Richard Dreyfuss
even if he writes fine poems? And despite
protestations that they had to leave, they stayed.
Actually, I think I really met him two days later
when I read the poems for the third time,
letting my hand move across the page like his,
keeping time with the cadence of the words—
and suddenly I felt like *davening,* though I'm
not Jewish, and women—well, at the Portuguese
Synagogue in Amsterdam we were banished
to the balcony behind a Moorish grille, to see
but not be seen, as if the pungent essence
of temptation couldn't filter through the filigree.
Yes, I felt like *davening,* because I sensed
something beyond his words and my voice,
beyond the immediacy of his experience, something
underlying even Emily Dickinson's white dress
in the poem I was reading aloud, and I could see
his ancestor, an old grandfather, a rabbi, perhaps,
in a broad-brim hat, the fringes of his white *tallis*
tangled like Mary Pickford curls below the hem
of his black serge coat. I could see the old man's
beard falling in chiseled waves as though
Michelangelo had had a hand in it, see him standing
there, swaying back and forth, chanting psalms

that had been handed down from father to father to
son, and I could see his hand, his left hand,
extended over the prayer book as if greeting
each sacred word, but moving deftly
like a reflection of the poet, moving from
right to left and back again, from right to left.

—for Marvin Bell

A Quasi-Saint in Two (or Three) Acts

Remembering Virgil Thomson

1. *Saint John the Too-Too Divine*

Dwarfed in this cavernous tribute to God
we sing your praises. Everybody's here,
Virgil, even the dead. You'd have loved this—
though you claimed you were fussed over only
because you lived so *long*, hanging around,
till the only thing left for us to do
was to honor you, again . . . and again.
"In my family," you once confided
to the world, "we don't die; we do fall down,"
the TV lens catching a glimpse of grin,
then panning to reveal a cherubic
old man in a smoking jacket, propped up
in a green stuffed chair, rows and rows of books
and art supporting the walls of your life.
And now, you—our lusting, listing angel,
sepulchered, skewered, though not quite snuffed—
drawl greetings from the other side. We can't
seem to shed you, Virgil—you remain here,
ever here, ever best, father/mother
of us all—we've gotten used to you, friend,
and we're reluctant to give up the ghost.

2. *Parting Words*

A soprano sings us a final song,
Gertrude's words, your music, resonating
in this deep, dark mouth of heaven—*Listen!*
she says, and we do: *We cannot retrace*
our steps, we do not retrace our steps. All
my long life. I start to cry. *And here, here*
we are here in marble and gold—did I

say gold?—yes I said gold—marble and gold.
I study my hands. When I look up, I
see my ex-husband—the link between us—
standing in the dim nave, weeping also.
He waves, but I am loath to share my loss
with him. *We do not retrace our steps.*

(3. *Death Makes Strange Bedfellows*

They say celebrities die in threes—and
little did you suspect your threesome would
embrace Bette Davis and Irving Berlin—
though you, yourself, were a Davis of sorts,
oft-quoted, bitchy; your indisputable
wit brimming with mischief, bridging the
ages. You, too, were a bumpy ride—one
not knowing who'd bear the brunt of your next
"sassy but classy" foray. Hemingway
remained a favorite target throughout
the century—"Women," you'd begin with
great amusement, "were always after him"
(pause) "but they never stayed" (pause, again), then
after looking around, you'd add, "*nobody*
ever saw him without his clothes on."
As the night and wine wore on, nobody
saw Ravel without *his*—or, for that matter,
Gertrude without *hers*.
With Berlin you
had in common America, each in
your own way celebrating the grandeur
of her mountains, her wheat fields, her rivers.
You wanted Paris to know Kansas City,
to understand "how we feel on the banks
of the Kaw and the Missour-ah." You felt
there was a similarity between
the two cities: "They've both got lots of

religion, good food, and general
corruption around."
                        But what you loved most
about America was her spirit—
the spunk, drive, and humor of her people,
virtues you, Bette, and Irving embodied.
And you could afford to laugh, you three—and
laugh you did—you outlived everybody!)

Italicized words in Part 2 are from "My Long Life," the closing song of the Virgil Thomson-Gertrude Stein opera, *The Mother of Us All.*

Velcro

Because the truth
of your discovery will never
be aired, I sing to you, Mother,
collector of cockles and burrs,
their tight-fisted claws clutching
the hem of your slacks
like my fingers the back
of your skirt as I followed you
across my childhood, protesting
your hasty departures,
long absences. They stick
to you now as I did then—
tears flowing from the tear
of separation—their
tiny mouths oozing, oozing.

I salute you, my mother,
salute your fine eye, quick turn
of fate as you transformed
mishap into high invention,
assembling those bristly outcasts
into a renegade band of usefulness
destined to rival Edison & company
with its queer, cheery resonance—

khrrrrrrksh, khrrrrrksh

I praise you, Mother, gatherer
of natural ideas that stuck
and stick to you like, yes, velcro,
but before velcro became velcro
when it was still a startled clump
of thorns prickling the smooth surface
of your imagination, spurring you on
to wild associative leaps of chance

and possibility, taking you
a jump further than an arabesque—
beyond the now, the is—
into a futuristic stage of make believe
and quick costume changes,
where you could shift identities in
split-seconds: flamenco to
Hindu to rhumba to jazz
in dances choreographed
by Herbert Ross before
he became Herbert Ross—
dances low and muscular and sexy
that kept you out of the stuffy
Palmer House, but led you
across the many stages of life,
two-second changes thrown in
to ease the way, slow
the fall, the ever-present fall,
skulking in the wings.

And, oh, those burrs, Mother,
gripping and stripping in the blink
of an eye, perfect suitors—
caring, complacent, coming always
to your rescue, and singing
your unfurled song

khrrrrrrksh, khrrrrrksh

like a heart tearing apart
again and again,
showing its wild, raw wound
to the world.

Abbott's Scar

spills like a road map from his heart:
two blue tracks, centimeters apart,
divide the pale landscape of his torso.
He smiles, unbuttons one story
at a time—slowly, seductively—
determined to bring each one
to a happy conclusion. The roads
begin below the clavicle, parallel
each other, converge, split apart,
converge again like errant skis
ending in a pile-up just above the belt.
I trace their paths, the saga
of chance: knee shattered
on an out-of-the-way ski slope,
a blood clot breaking loose
ten years later like a bad memory,
invading a lung, then flaking off
like the powder snow that lures us on
and often gets the better of us,
no matter how well we plan each trip,
make the right arrangements,
arrive on time, pay all the bills.
There's always an untrodden route
beckoning to us from the side of logic,
promoting this or that thrill,
this or that adventure. And we
take it each time, trusting our skill,
tasting our courage, testing our luck.

A Gift from the Poet

I am reading a poem by Gerald Stern
and I hear his voice—though in truth I've never
heard his voice—and I see his mouth clearly, like
Chaucer's lisping Wife's, though, again, I've never
seen his mouth. And I'm uneasy, it all seems
too familiar: the full lips, the gap between
the teeth, the voice thick, a bit raspy, tobacco
staining its vowels. And the eyes in this face
that started out as Stern's are milky blue, skimmed
of cream, like mother's milk that turns the morning
coffee gray and thin, and like Picasso's they
bulge with secrets only he and I seem to
remember—who could this be that I know yet
do not know? Bartok, he writes, was dying when
he composed his last and best concerto. He
told no one—not a soul. So brave. So alone.
Yes, it's coming to me slowly. I can sense
it in the cadence of the words, see it as
the poet sits cross-legged and bent beneath
his silken shawl, sits as Bartok must have sat,
humble but undefeated, coaxing the life
to transcend itself into a work of art,
the art into a life. It's coming now a
little faster, taking form like the poem
itself, leading me beyond the poet's words,
down a dim hall, paper gaping on the walls,
inarticulate flowers waving me on
to revive each vacant room, give voice to what
was—what must have been!—in this second or third
adopted haven. I run to the end of
the hall where a door, the last door, swings open
and there, in the dull yellow kitchen—my heart
hopscotching across the brick linoleum—
there, at last, I find him, an old friend. He sits
at the table, his hands cupping his head—a

heavy head, round and smooth and infinitely beautiful. He looks up, smiles, motions to me to join him. Shamelessly, I eat his supper.

—Remembering Sue's father, Robert Fish

Bach's Augmented Ninth

In the bass line
of a piano piece
my daughter is learning
one hand at a time
I hear a familiar theme.

Cramped there
for contrapuntal purpose
it is to soar
generations later
over the Finnish landscape.

Leipzig is small, compact
a perfect cameo.
Finland remains untamed
untapped
augmented tenfold and
like Sibelius
reaching beyond invention.

—for Anika

Wizardry

—for Dorothy Coulter Hall

These people don't know your voice
is the color of Venice at dusk.
No one has taught them to listen. Here
in this taco joint, while you sing an aria
to an old friend whose ruby-sequined
espadrilles reflect the shimmer
of your song, they joke and shout
commands for hot sauce and tequila.
When I comfort you, you shrug and say,
"I think I was given a voice so someday
when I'm old and dotty I can entertain
the folks in the nursing home."
Somehow, it is fitting you should end up
in a Kansas townhouse over what
was once a farm, tornados raging back
and forth over the tomatoes and corn,
razing the living, raising the dead.
All passion in the land. Though never
did you dream your career would spin
itself out in the eye of silence.
Still, in this Kansas suburb your voice
radiates like a prairie fire,
the sounds vital, pure, consoling,
as they spread from Mozart to Oz to us.

An Act of Love

—In memory of Bob Townsend who
brought us bread at Christmas

"Some get high on drugs,
my satori is bread."
—from the film, "Diva"

I smell fresh bread—
yeast, I think you said—
and remember you always
in the act of kneading,
your fingers pleading
with the dough, coaxing
it into fleshy breasts

and thighs, then pressing
down, flattening it out
with the heel of your hand,
then breast again until
it resists your will,
holds together like skin.

To make bread, you said,
is a blessing, a way
of coming to grips with God,
with dread. To give bread
is an offering of love,
bearing with it
the smell of the earth and
of the baker. I feel

that, too, as I push and
pull the taffy-like dough,

kneading it until it doubles
in size, triples, grows
so huge it can feed
the multitude, feed the soul,

bring back the dead.

III

Caprichos tiene la sed . . .
—Antonio Machado

Shadows & Supposes

On a train, going backward, I watch
what I've already passed, see what's
about to appear superimposed on
my husband's glasses. The world melds
into a wild collage: steeples bridge

evergreens, skies tear mountains apart
with their eyes, rococo gargoyles claw
my back, float like Chagall goats over
mansard roofs and crenelated towers.
I want to preserve each moment—my life,

like the photos I take, layered with innuendo,
possibility curtsying in a three-way mirror
at some unlived yet remembered dream.
Myths, Sagan calls them, those things
that never happened, yet are and always

will be—and here I am, neither myth
nor mythmaker, speeding backward from
my ancestor the mite to some assignation
in the future when what's about to come
might have already come and gone.

Night on the Town

1.
At my 40th high school reunion
the names of the missing
are the only ones I remember.
The people in charge are strangers.
My name is not among the missing.

2.
A crowded bar, frenetic
music with someone else's words.
The waitress presses against you.
She's young. Unattractive.
It doesn't matter what she looks like.

3.
The fat man like a Botero painting
leans against the afternoon, surveys
the scene, his beer-bottle eyes
caressing the single women
at the bar. *FBI*, you whisper.

4.
The poet at our table lurches
forward, yells the secret of life
over his half-eaten cheeseburger.
The music drowns out his words.

5.
Through the filigree partition
a woman confesses: men love her only
when they are alone with her—
in curtained rooms, transoms
locked, flowers crowding their
soundproofed vows.

6.
In his mind she is all mouth,
a cove, inviting, like his first
pillow rolled up between
his thighs, deep as vowels,
firm as trust.

7.
In her mind he is all mouth,
tongue on her lips, neck, cheeks,
breasts, etc. (etc.
always the best part)—warm,
heady, sleek as a ruse.

8.
In her mouth he is all mind.

9.
She washes inside and out, makes sure
everything vital is neutralized.
He lies on his back. Dreams.

10.
She is naked. He looks
past her, reaches behind her
for his coat, his sleeve grazing
her nipple. A gash of moonlight
slashes her in two.

11.
This morning I fell into your dream:
you were mounting another woman,
riding her into the moonless night.
I screamed *giddyap* and buried
my spur into her rump.

12.
A mourning dove coos its mournful
song across the meadow.
In a moment another dove answers.
The coos greet each other on the 16th green,
size each other up, embrace, become
entangled, knotted, enslaved, distraught,
despairing.

13.
Everything is crystal clear.
Through the empty glasses I see them
whispering secrets into their open palms.
When they close their hands in a fist
they clutch plastic flowers.

new shoes and an old flame

shopping today i see a pair of kinky
yves st. laurent
shoes and
think of you
now why do you
suppose my mind
not unlike bubble
gum pushed to its
very limits springs
back upon your image
sticking to the thought
of you wondering how
you'd feel about those
skinny call-girl heels cause
i'm still   coming on to you
you see   even though i
tell my-   self you're gone
now one   of those people we
speak   of with reverence or
a hint   of smile suggesting something
deeper   than we ever let on   your name
still   makes me smile and think of
high-   heel shoes—the higher, the better

Cardinal Rule

Even the female is striking,
flaming orange beak and crest,
long red-tipped tail feathers
motioning up and down, and

up and down, like the slow
steady finger of Mae West
beckoning to Cary Grant in that
old movie they used to show

at the Thalia, and though
it was in black and white
you just knew the tips
of her fingers were sparks,

matching her searing lips,
entreating all will—Shakespeare's
kind—to rise and make a stab
at it. Small wonder Britons

call their women *birds*. Arabs,
on the other hand, conspiring
to keep passion under wraps,
swathe their women in black—

and still they stun you
with a quick glance, desire
escaping like fire from their
kohl eyes. It seems whatever

the shade of her feathers, or
however the male perceives his role,
it's the female of the species
who fans the coals.

Visitations

He wakes her.
Every night he wakes her
as if afraid her dreams will take her
take her to a world she will prefer
to his. He cannot stop himself
cannot stop from muttering
words so low only she can hear them
words so low they sneak in undetected
under the closed door of sleep
slipping in like uninvited guests
who sit and wait to be attended.
She pretends to ignore them
but cannot erase their stormy presence
in her story, a story of a dream
within the dream, a dream
of corridors, of doors opening and
closing on thin shrieks of light
that hiss demands across
the dreary night. Each night
she must respond, respond with
words so low only he can hear them
words so low they seep in undetected
bruising his own locked dream.
And so it goes, night after night
dream after dream
first one and then the other
until the first light wakens them
wakens them both to silence.

Fowl Play

Our argument last night survives my silence.
Today, in a tenuous truce, we stroll down
the Venice canal—unusually muddy,
yesterday's water gurgling below the surface
like our accusations, buried but yielding
an odd assortment of treasure and trash.
We stop to watch the shore birds—gulls, herons,
egrets, a couple of marbled godwits—scramble
for something more, something else to sate
their hunger, and suddenly a brawl breaks out
between the gulls and the egrets. The great blue,
caught in the middle of the squall,
elegant, long-legged, its hair free-flowing like
a southern California fern, shuffles away,
its head bobbing on its curved neck, forward and
back, forward and back, to an inner blues beat
that drowns out the raucous cawing around it.
I smile at our own novice anger—ingenues
in a blue movie, who can't quite get it on
(what my husband dreamt the night before—only
in his dream it was someone else's wife who'd fled
in search of passion, fled from "the handsomest
guy in the class"—even beauty has no hold
on fealty—*in sickness and in health* be damned!).
We marvel at this snapping, flapping, screeching
confrontation, the great blue keeping its head
and its distance, as I tried last night to keep mine.
The birds scatter, but the cries continue. When
I look closely I see that all that noise is coming
from a single ring-billed gull, puffed up, angry,
squatting in the mud, screaming his heart out.

Ode to Your Back

The days wrap themselves around me
like worn shawls.
I am cold, always
on the point of shivering.

Nights come stunted and maimed,
undernourished children
with no place to go.

This night I dream of happy
endings: the hero, turbaned, rouged,
made up with heart-shaped lips, penciled
brows, married to the ingenue
to keep her safe because he loves
is not in love with her and

wake to find us, you and me
and the war-orphaned babies in London
who died from lack of touch
and my own chilled body moving,
moving in close to the heat

of your back. Your back.

Smitten

He tells me her house is full
of mousers, fat and cunning, and
that you can't get past the foul
smell and that his eyes swell up
like radishes in spring and that
he wheezes and his nose drips and
how can her poor husband stand it?
Hmmmm. I remember once falling
for a man with hair like limp
spaghetti, teeth the color of turnips,
and six-pack-flavored breath:
his socks drooped around his shoes
like soggy onion rings and I knew
I could never love a man who
looked like that. Not ever. So what
does it matter if he says he loathes
cats or if her eyes are too small
and close together and her nose
bears to the right as though it's
pressed against a wish or if her voice
is flat as a Kansas wheat field
after a tornado, without a breeze,
without a tumbleweed, without
so much as the sound of a cowbell.
It means nothing. And his visits
have grown longer, more frequent, and
he comes home late, singing out of tune,
cat hairs clinging to his lapels.

The Size of Love

She knew she had lost him the night he flew
back from St. Paul and whispered
in her hair while they were making love
"You're so small . . . so small . . ." She knew
in that instant how much wider
the summer arc of his arms had been.

She could feel her body compensating
for his loss, feel it broaden and
lengthen like clay beneath his weight,
taking on needed dimension
to make up for what it lacked in June.

She grew. Oh, how she grew! Her buttocks
ripened into an Arab's dream, cassavas.
Her breasts swelled like dunes
beneath his breath. Trellised with
oleander her hair burst into flame,
her plainsong into laughter. And soon,
beside herself with newfound love
of self, she answered to another name.

Somapsychosis

He said it softly
almost inaudibly
letting it slide in
between the maybe and but
of diagnosis.
She pretended not to hear
afraid the few antinuclear
antibodies
invading her blood
would bond with her psyche
and vanquish
the but and maybe
she could cling to.

Something was possibly wrong.

But as long
as it had no name
it had no life, she thought—
until she got home
that night and, like an
errant child commanded,
wrote the word
over and over and over again,
until the punishment
took hold.

Janus

She knows a man
whose hands stay
in his head, whose lips
lie behind his eyelids,
whose words splinter in
his throat. His heart stews in
a dark liquid. When he sighs
bubbles surface and disperse
into the inarticulate night.
When he growls, as he must
from time to time, the
earth quakes and
all the gremlins lost
in the nether world
emerge and rage.

I know a man
whose heart is clear
as water, whose gifts
float to the surface
like lifeboats on missions
of mercy. He disseminates
hope. When he laughs
his mirth rises from the deep
in riotous geysers of ginger
and gold. And when he loves,
oh, his words calm the sea,
position themselves
in the night sky and
sing us, one by one,
into his galaxy.

Locks: A Cautionary Tale

> "Some 20,000 king salmon were killed during the opening day ceremony for John Day Dam in 1968. . . . The ceremony, however, was a big success."
>
> —Joe Upton, "On Western Waters"

The engines pause at one A.M., again
at four A.M., then shut down—like your snores
when at night you loose all breath, the silence
shocking me awake, an alarm going
off in my delta sleep nudging me to
nudge you alive again—and I sit up
in bed fully alert, bumped by the boat's
rude bounce off the concrete wall of the dam,
the river beneath us dropping more than
one hundred feet in fifteen minutes, dropping
to greet its downstream equal when the lock
will rise slowly above us, high above
the waves, allowing us to venture down
the Snake and the Columbia, down toward
Cape Disappointment, like those two madmen
who mapped their way into our future and
our past, melding their dreams into this mess
of destiny and history, this illusion
of progress that silenced the salmon, the falls
and the rivers we navigate today,
step by step, with awe and trepidation.

Trout Fishing Off Captiva Island

—for Jane

I've been rooting for the fish all
afternoon, when I get a bite
and suddenly, I'm excited
as hell—not expecting to be,
somewhat ashamed—but excited
nonetheless, excited by the tug,
his, then mine, then his again. I
feel betrayed by my own hunger,
alarmed at how I jump to meet
this smallest challenge. My guide
shouts a rhythmic reminder to

slack, jerk, pull,
slack, jerk, pull—*reel*

He points out a baby trout on
my line thrashing against the hull
of the boat and it reminds me
of my baby sister throwing
herself against the pavement the
one time my mother harnessed her
to keep her from harm. She bolted
and I knew the sense of freedom
she was after, having grown up
surrounded by iron walls and
wills too treacherous to scale—

reel—*reel!*

the guide commands and I reel—
faster, tighter, the pole digging
its angry stump into my hip,
my hand stuttering at the fifth,

eighth, eleventh ungainly turn.
This fish don't wanna die, he laughs,
and again I see my sister
thrashing her tethered body against
our mother's yielding sternness—
instinctively my arm relaxes,
the lure shooting like spit across
the water—then the line goes slack—

real slack.

En Route II

Through an opening in the clouds
I can see my mother returning to her bed,
her head swollen with questions I cannot
answer: Did she say the wrong thing?
Do the wrong thing? Was the visit
a success? I cannot comfort her, cannot
tell her what she wants to hear, and
she will not hear what I have to tell her—
we are each intent on dying, dying
in our own way—her body by degrees,
my mind in one sudden flip-flop
when last night I looked out the rear
window and saw no escape, only
another window across the way bathed
in an eerie crimson light. What to make
of these epiphanies, these occasional
coalescences of perception?—the coffee
cools as before, the blood clots, or doesn't.
Would you like some juice? the flight
attendant whines in a voice too brazen
for the subtlety of the horizon, its amber
hues easing out the night, subduing
the creases on my mother's ambiguity
as she bids me farewell and wonders, as
I do, if we shall ever see each other again.
I drew a map for my sleeping daughter
revealing the key to her inheritance—
Never let your children see you naked,
the old ones counsel, and they remain
silent, hiding assets, hoarding pills,
poisons, ways out. But what would I *do*
with their clutched secrets, where

would I take them?—my future
precarious at best: 37,000 feet in the air,
with no parachute, no wings,
not even the illusion of a prayer.

Acrobatics

I envy the squirrel leaping
effortlessly from limb to limb

and never missing—connecting
sometimes only by the very

tip of claw, but weighing nothing,
so nothing to draw it earthward,

shuddering. Instead, like a wisp
of down wind-plucked from the throat of

flight it breaks free, falls free, risks all,
legs outstretched like divining rods

reaching for sustenance, gambling
between earth and sky, life and death,

between what is and what might be.

The Ghosts of Martha's Vineyard

Of what is past, or passing, or to come.
—Yeats

Strange flight East. Meet a woman
from L.A. en route to Boston
who will one day betray me.
Man on my left sells Japanese beer,
leans toward me revealing secrets
of where to eat in Hong Kong,
though I have no intention of ever
going to Hong Kong, and of his friend
my friend Malcolm Frager with whom
he'd stay on his way to somewhere
carrying his little black bag
that slips neatly under the seat
in front of him. Miller was wrong:
they never die, these salesmen,
but divide and subdivide into invading
armies of regulars securing airports
nightclubs, hotels. Never concert halls
or museums. Never bookstores.

We change to a toy plane in Boston.

I smell the ocean before the door
opens and that part of me languishing
in Middle America rejoices, lifts me
from my seat and throws me
into an old friend's arms. He smiles,
en corné, gilded bullhorns flopping comically
on his royal blue cap. We trade hats.

Our host bellows hello from a white
crisp country kitchen—David, ever
the graduate in yellow shetland pullover,
loud smile, indestructible teeth,
warm celtic blue eyes. He takes me

shshhsshhing on tiptoe to where
the tiniest baby dolls slumber—
beneath mushrooms, green leafy parasols,
behind books, under chairs, their naked
plastic bodies frozen in sleep.
Under microscopic eyes they weep
real tears for me because I'm mortal.

This was Katherine Cornell's house,
Chip-Chop, wide, woody, weathered,
with a horizontal view of marsh and
sky that sweeps like two brush strokes
across the world, a filtered world,
the light pearled, ladylike, unlike
Santa Fe, where it presses straight
down on you with a whorish persistence.

In the distance moon-high osprey nests
hinge the sky to the earth.

The living room, theatrically rustic,
seems familiar, as if we'd all been
here before—perhaps a *mise en scène*
in a Noel Coward play: Kit Cornell,
shoulders padded, sharing a moment
on stage with Raymond Massey, Noel
watching from the wings, waiting to go on
and steal the show, yes; and
he would have played the stunted piano
in the corner, a premature baby grand,
out of tune with time, and they all
would have gathered round singing
clever songs about their clever friends—
change the names, we're all still here.

David disappears into another set
in this fictitious house. But first
he must show me everything: the two

kitchens, one somber, one sublime;
the bath I'm to share with this run's
cast of neo-Coward characters;
Kit's room with the famous Death Bed
where I'm to sleep—and as though
to balance this moribund plot, he
has placed a pot of purples on the sill:
a splash of passion at odds
with the bed's and the bogs' austerity.

Last of all, he shows me
the writing alcove, and there,
half-hidden on the topmost shelf of a hutch,
above the books and typewriter,
beyond the present, perhaps the future,
bulging and pregnant, ribbon-tied and mute,
the only things we may not touch:
manila folders bearing secret letters
from Helen Keller.

                    Kit's former companion
comes by that night to tell us stories
about Helen, brilliant Helen, who soon
outgrew the giving mind and hand
of Annie. Curious Helen, attending
all of Cornell's plays, her tireless
teacher at her side transmitting action,
dialogue, style of costume, sets—
all, all into Helen's hungry palm.

Tell me, tell me, tell me.
Speak to me of ecstasy, speak to me of love.

And the prophet Annie spoke—but
what would she have said of love? Would
she have helped Helen "snatch light
out of darkness"? "A hand has made me,
fashioned me, and molded my very soul,"

Helen wrote. "To me it meant
knowing a life, instead of living a death."

Tell me, touch me, hold me.

And I here now sense longings.
And I here now sense unutterable longings
lurking in the shutters, in the books,
in the snapshots of Vineyard
afternoons, woven into the wicker framing
our small talk a generation later,
splintered in the floorboards we weather
with our steps as we skitter from trinket
to trinket, touching, stroking,
laying hands as Helen must have—Oh yes,

ineffable longings lying in pink abandon
like the tiny silent babies David
planted throughout the house, the lawn—

lying in wait—

on this umbral Vineyard afternoon.

—for David Stickelber

Final Cut

—after seeing Ingmar Bergman's "Fanny and Alexander"

They are never the same, the dream
and the ritual retelling.
The daimonic has no equal in
translation. All craft falls short—tame,

tepid as a melting clock on canvas.
How can the forger not suffer,
knowing illusion gels this side of terror,
knowing that sleight of hand is slight at best?

Still, time and again—fast forward, slow
reverse, panning, or zooming in—he
will persist in stalking eternity,
holding and closing on its long shadow,

splitting its echo with his claim
and risking all he's got for one final
shot at fame—or is it immortality?—knowing all
the while he's doomed to miss it by a frame

or more. And potent though his vision may seem
to others, vagueness taunts his dream.

Reflections

A woman sits in her car,
the window down
despite the rain,

a street lamp revealing
the curved crescent
of arm, neck,

the stark pale grace
of a question unasked,
unanswered. She leans

forward slightly,
as if to find a better angle
in the glass façade,

and I—observer, subject,
stranger—marvel at
this apparition, wait

for the light to change,
before proceeding
with caution.

IV

"Sin in its exaggerated form became an obsessional neurosis, a paranoid combination of perfectionism and narcissism connecting death and crime, sin and punishment. At its root there is *mad love.*"

—Jean Delumeau, *Sin and Fear*

The Fall

And yet another ode to fall and falling,
another tribute to October light,
to bushes burning in defiance of night,
to Monet, Seurat. Ah, but not until

you've seen an Ozark autumn, not until
then can you understand the plight of Eve,
can you fathom passion, blasphemy.
Apples red, ready, *blur* beside the sensuous

leaf about to fall.
                    Yes, she must have sensed
the beauty of the consequence—else why
bite into shame? The promise of gold obscures
all reason, good intentions, God—luring

us into the daze of earthly glitter,
into the pyre (is that then what it's all
about—gold and ashes?), into blazing
in a moment of orgasmic fury—

and *dying*—
            if only to create fire.

In the Crevices of Night

There's a man in my dream
a man with a hatchet
ransacking my bureau
hacking at the doll asleep
in the bottom drawer.

A bloodless ritual.

He calls himself a surgeon, says
he's up on the latest laser beam
techniques. I know better.
I know the jig's up.
Youth is waning and the end
is closing in on the beginning—
a telescopic fantasy focused
on dismembered limbs, a glass eye
rolling across the parquet floor,
tiny fingernails scattered
in my underwear scratching
at the obscenity of early death.
But not a drop of blood. Not a cry.

I turn from the dream
and pressing my body to yours
reach for you
across the thin ice of night.

Lydia's Phantasmagoria

And tonight's headline news:
All of Puerto Rico watches as TV's Queen of Soaps
is condemned to life imprisonment. Stay tuned.

High,
like when you're in a glass elevator going up
and you feel stationary
and everything around you seems to be going down,
dropping,
slipping slowly away:
the light switch slinking down the wall, the vase
full of flowers sinking beneath the painting
over the mantel, the Ralph Goings painting of a woman—
could be any woman, though he calls her Shanna,
sitting at a Kentucky Fried Chicken window booth—
a woman left suddenly, left alone,
left incomplete as though half of her had fallen
away, disappeared out of sight,
the two cups of coffee on the table unsipped,
growing clotted and cool like the relationship,
the cigarette between her fingers
no longer sparkling, but smouldering imperceptibly
like the one who left, is left,
and the cross-legged woman left behind reworks,
rephrases the parting words,
restructures, relives the final scene,
repossesses what may or may not have been said (she
can't remember), so that it hurts less,
maybe even comes out right
with a musical comedy ending of forever
and ever amen and all that crap and *caramba.*

But it's not that way—not that time,
not this time, not then, not now, not ever, and
the word that can heal gets mislaid, misfired,
feelings misstated, misconstrued,
justice miscarried, sometimes all the way to the chair,
and not the one looking out from
Colonel Sanders' place—that's art, that's fiction;
this is life, death. This is murder.

In the beginning . . . hell, there is no beginning,
only a question and answer period to start
and the questions are loaded and the answers are invariably wrong
and these two, like the couple in the Goings painting,
they tried—we all try.
The story goes (and I have no reason to doubt it)
that Lydia did him in—
one night while making love—a long time coming round,
too long—Luis made the fatal slip, calling her
by the other one's name.
Had she still been in the throes of ecstasy
his *Nydia* might have sneaked by undetected,
but as patience would have it, she heard,
stiffened beneath him,
her body hard and flat and dry;
his, finally spent, sprawling like a lead sheet
across the glass bones of her rage—and
in that moment
she knew he had deceived her
and knowing,
waited,
waited until the time was right,
playing at the game of love while playing for time,

not yet knowing what to do
but knowing something had to be done, someone
done in.
She plotted in the only way she knew—Dantesquely
fitting the punishment to the crime.
She hired three (already a mistake, a stupid mistake,
3 x 2 = 6 too many
involved, too many palms to grease,
bucks to pass) thugs, hired three thugs to kill him.
But first the slow revenge—intense,
steady—because death after all is liberation,
slow revenge is pain: an imprisonment of self
within self, a double jeopardy of torture.
Satisfied, she rubbed her hands with wicked glee
and laughed *¡Ja! ¡Ja!* adding
the Spanish equivalent of "you bastard, you'll moan
and groan for *me* before I'm through!" (*Hijo de la gran . . .* etcetera.)

On January 6th the three thugs—kings for a day—
kidnapped him and delivered him blindfolded
to a nondescript, out-of-the-way room
in a bourgeois suburb of San Juan
that smelled of *chorizos* and *habichuelas*.
Miramar without a view—no ocean, no sky, no moon, no place
for the reigning stars of Puerto Rican soaps to be caught dead in.
And, waiting for him, his patient wife—
legs crossed, cigarette smouldering like the one
in the painting—eye ready behind
an instantaneously gratifying
Kodakcolorpolaroid,
its protruding flashbulb palpitating
like a stud in heat—ready to document the brilliant defeat
of Luis in particular, man in general, ready to

show him falling from dignity,
from hope, from grace,
from the top of the popularity polls (*click!*)
falling (*click!*) to ignominy and low, low ratings.
And she ascending on that elevator
getting high, higher,
snapping and flashing
picture (*click!*) after picture
of his long, slow descent.
He might have stepped backwards out of an open window
on the 31st floor of the CBS building
and fallen to his death in 5 and 9/10ths of a second,
but instead he was snapped up,
snapped over and over again, his wounds hissing
in vivid color,
his tiny parts removed one by one—
a nail (*click!*), an earlobe (*click!*),
a testicle (*click! click! click! click! click!*)—missing
except in the snapshots strewn face up
across the blood-soaked bittersweet shag carpet.
And Luis missing the good lines,
missing the applause—
Oh baby missing you-oo-oo-oo, oh baby missing you-hooo-oo—
missing all but the last laugh—
between *socorros* (Pietá never had it so good)
he damned her and cursed her and spited her
with cries for Nydia! Nydia! Nydia!
which sounded to her like the *nya-nya-nyaaaah*
of vengeful siblings,
and suddenly Lydia felt his anguish, his anger.
Saw his hatred.
And to shut out a reflection of her own loathsomeness,
she ordered the three assassins

to pluck out his eyes (*click! click!*).
Nearly out of film she had them stuff his body
into his car, douse it with gasoline,
set it on fire. Strains of *aguinaldos* drifted in
through the open window—*abrir la puerta al niño*
que está pidiendo amparo . . . etcetera.

Steadying the camera on the second-story window ledge,
the craggy bricks carving deep ridges into her elbows,
she snaps the final spectacle from above.
And Lydia becomes the flames—
teasing, playful, at first—her fingers
combing the fringes of the orange floral bedspread,
pulling off each petal—
he loves me, he loves me not—
unfolding each leaf, each bud, her tongue
reading his skin like Braille—every pore,
every mole, every tangled curl telling a different story,
spelling a new name—
he loves her, he loves me not.
As the flames rise
higher and higher past her window
she tilts the camera up toward the soiled sky,
and all at once she feels herself sinking
irreversibly
as though she were on an elevator
plummeting
through the earth's mantel,
deep, deep into the magma of memory,
beyond hope, beyond redemption, beyond *revision*,
watching everything,
everything she had ever wanted,
everything she had ever loved, evanesce—

watching her whole life
go up in smoke.

Trailer: *Tune in next week to the first episode*
of Love and Murder: On Screen and Off, *featuring*
that hot new sensation Nydia Estrella,
in the title role of Lydia (click! click! click!).

---

socorros: cries for help
habichuelas: beans
aguinaldos: Christmas carols
abrir la puerta al niño que está pidiendo amparo: open the door to the child begging for shelter

Knife

She was old. She lived alone in a small house
two blocks away. When they found her, days after,
she had been stabbed seventeen times—as if
a host of assassins had struck an empress down.
She even might have looked up briefly
before the final cut, spurting blood and
an imperious last line or two. Perhaps not.
Perhaps the first wound had done the trick—
the rest sport for the mad or wicked. A handyman
lived nearby. He worked odd jobs while leading
a secret life with his neighbor's Anglo wife,
who would sneak him in when her husband
and her son were out. No one questioned
Sánchez about the old lady. He traveled alone.
This was a gang job. One day while walking past
a vacant lot close by, the boy spots a shiny
object winking at him through layers of rust
like a cheap sequin—summoning him to stoop
down, swoop it up, later to brandish it
with pride before his mother's sucked
astonishment. *Give it here,* she says.
The name on the crudely carved handle is clear,
letters printed in black Magic Marker—but
are they clearly the handyman's? Sánchez
is a common name. She knows he doesn't stand
a chance if he stands trial. Knows they'll find
guilt hidden like stacks of money unexplained
beneath the floorboards of his mind. She knows
Texas. Knows how stuff gets planted when you're
a Mexican without an alibi and they need
a solution. And most of all she knows, knows
as she digs the tiny grave for the homemade knife,

knows as she pats the soil over it and sows
the seeds of justice, knows as she pours
a 50-50 mixture of water and fish emulsion
over it to make the seeds grow, knows, damn it,
she just knows that he is guilty as hell.

Mixed Media Event, or Heavy Stuff

—for Sasson Soffer

Someday it's going to fall
on me that painting on the wall
over my bed and I'll be decapitated
by eighty-six pounds of
ultramarine and viridian acrylic
framed in gold-leaf strips.
When my husband returns
from one of his business trips,
he'll think it quite a trick
to find a Segal-like stiff
protruding from a 2-D work of art—
trick indeed that he was out of town
when the guillotine came down.

But so it is in life as well as bed:
while one is losing his heart
another may be losing her head.

The Falconer Ties His Mate to the Block

He keeps a short rein on her,
showering her with beepers,
cell phones, walkie-talkies,
so when he casts her off, her
primaries can only take her
so far—the lure, the quarry,
mere illusions he flushes
for her edification. He is master,
wielding the bow net, wearing
the gauntlet. When he whistles
she returns at once, offering
her slim ankles one at a time
for the jesses, her head bowed
for the hood. At home
he's installed an elaborate
intercom so he can hear her
breathe, hear her bate,
hear her sizzle as she screams
through the night air, spiraling
with him in her dreams.

Ronda

On Tuesday they moved my father's
body from its temporary quarters
run by the state to a private plot
on the outskirts of San Juan. "Not

too far away," my sister assures me.
"When you come this summer we'll
visit. I think you'll like it better."
My stepmother spent the year

making *coquito* out of coconut
milk and rum. She sold enough bottles
at Christmas to raise the $350 it cost
to move my father's body across

town. I marvel at her zeal,
but think, too, of his impending ordeal,
of his bones having to make fresh
indentations in the soil, his flesh

having to warm the land around him.
Even in death he seems condemned
to suffer life's transgressions—
forced to break in a final mattress,

to take in a final mistress.

Father's Day

This time his father takes him
to the Liberty Memorial,
a World War I monument
overlooking the city. In single
file they climb the spiral
staircase, the boy's legs
straining to reach the last step.
Swell way to spend a Sunday,
his father had said, and
the boy feels proud to be
on top of the world with his dad.
The man leans over as if to kiss
him, the boy lifts his face
expectantly—suddenly he's upside
down and before he can resist
his father's fists around
his ankles he's dangling over
the side of the tower, dangling
like a tangled marionette above
the coaxing ground, his red
jacket, like a spurt of blood,
coating his head and arms as
they bang against the granite.
Coins from his pockets sprinkle
the earth with tiny setting suns.
You can always trust me, son—
his father's words bruise the air—
always, you hear? He feels
his heart pummeling his eyes
and ears, warm urine caressing
his chest. *Yes, Daddy, yes,*
he cries back, his voice threadbare

over the shivering treetops—
yes, yes—trying to penetrate
his father's glazed senses—
yes, yes—hoping to reassure him
once and for all, so he will stop
having to prove his love.

Bases Loaded

At
the
ballgame
people who
have never uttered
one kind word to one
another hug and kiss, hop up
and down, and scream with ethnic
abandon. Fans weep and blame each
other for losses they seem to feel more keenly
than death. A heavy-set woman in the third row
winds up and slugs her son because he shouts *hurray*
and claps his little hands when her shortstop fumbles. She is
oblivious of his pain at this first hit—the thud of bat against
ball, fist against skull fused in his future forever. The
woman next to my husband grabs his knee and
squeezes with the passion of a double. He
responds to the momentary pass by
squeezing back, his face flushed
with the anticipation of a
home run, the dread
of a triple play
just a batter
awa
y

Turning Point

he turns like milk
in a moment
no longer sweet
no longer palatable

who is this man
who turns
turns his back on me

children's faces
on the milk carton
smile at me
from the refrigerator shelf
faces from a time
that no longer exists
except in the family album
and on the waxed container
the milk inside
yellowed like old photos
sick tongues

were I to meet
these children now
I would not recognize
their faces
I would not understand
one word

Witness

The robins are blind drunk again,
the hawthorn tree just about bare.

They stagger through October air,
slam-dunk their bodies every now

and then into windowed versions
of themselves, sprawling stunned and

out of sorts on sill and deck—then
like good sports, hurting and dazed, they

rise and start again as though each
berry offered life not death. Two

blue jays on a nearby elm observe
the birds' debauchery like

wary relatives or friends shoved
to the sidelines of affection,

powerless to scold or coax or move
this other species that they love.

Home Free

My first husband
whose last words
to me were *pretend*
I'm dead
phones to tell me
our best friend
has died. He sobs,
apologizes for
being the bearer
of bad news.
Visions of ancient
Rome obs-
cure my sadness
and I smile at
his relentless
pursuit of danger.
Only after he hangs
up do I succumb
to sharing sorrow
with this now
twice-buried stranger.

Death in Love

". . . y el mejor bien es pequeño;
que toda la vida es sueño,
y los sueños sueños son."
—Pedro Calderón de la Barca

1.
In this room I cannot breathe. My
wheezes seem to come from other
selves: I am witness and victim.
Tiny valves in my heart conspire
against me. I clutch my throat like
Callas in Tosca, but I'm not
acting—I see death, feel its breath,
hear its rattle. It wears my clothes.

2.
Friends glide in and out of the room.
They are silent, as though I do
not suffer. I laugh at something
I hear in my head. No one smiles.
I tell myself to exhale, but
I'm afraid I'll remain breathless—
an empty cavity. Plaintive
chords of my organs comfort me.

3.
Rain pummels the skylight. I hear
the small sounds of objects being
lifted and replaced in the next room.
You've come back. I cry out: I've had
a nightmare! But before I can
recount my death in life, you speak.
When I am through, you keep silent
like the visitors in my sleep.

4.
Nightstorms come whether I'm awake
or sleeping. Death rings in my ears.
The weather of my dream is real:
my lungs warn of distant thunder,
my skin conjures rain. And the gloom?
Ah, the gloom! Like a sailor's caul
taut around my eyes, it casts its
merciful net over each life.

Taking the Long Way Home

You drive past a woman pushing a blue baby carriage,
her cheeks glowing with the pleasure of new motherhood, and
you smile, remembering—but in the rearview mirror you
catch her quickening her step, wiping her brow, glancing over
her shoulder—and you wonder if something is not quite right
with the scene, if her movements are not a bit off, her pace
not a bit frantic—and miles later you can see her still,
again and again, coming toward you, looking behind her,
as if someone were in pursuit, and you see that she is
agitated, her eyes dilated, her hair damp, matted,
her flowered dress clinging to her flesh, and that she's limping,
limping, her feet aching from having run several miles
before you first caught sight of her, before you smiled at her,
remembering—and you know now that the real mother is
lost somewhere in the dark inarticulate letters of
her daughter's name, unable to speak, unable to move,
unable to breathe—and you ask yourself why you didn't
stop, why you didn't stop the thieving woman in her tracks.

Back to Gotham

A distant figure in white weeps
across the prairie green of dawn
moving from left to right
like a searchlight from a helicopter
alerting the land of fugitives, drug deals,
abducted souls.

Birds have not yet revealed
their whereabouts. Night secrets
tryst in my head, seek
refuge in the palms of my hands.

At daybreak I'll be leaving
for that vertical city of stone and travertine
where an occasional beam of sunlight
reveals nothing

and no one ever gets found out.

Biographical Note

Gloria Vando is founding editor of Helicon Nine Editions, a literary small press in Kansas City, which for ten years published *Helicon Nine,* a journal of women's arts and letters, and currently publishes books. *Promesas: Geography of the Impossible,* her first book of poems, was a Walt Whitman finalist and won the Thorpe Menn Book Award. She is the coeditor of *Spud Songs: An Anthology of Potato Poems* (to benefit Hunger Relief) and editor of the *Helicon Nine Reader.* She received the first Artist Fellowship in poetry (1989) from the Kansas Arts Commission. Her poems have been included in many magazines and anthologies, and in several theatrical productions in New York City. Of Puerto Rican heritage, Vando was born and reared in New York City and educated in Amsterdam, Paris, and Texas. She now divides her time between Los Angeles and Kansas City.